D1716144

Animals on the Farm

by Joanne Ruelos Diaz illustrated by Simon Mendez

PICTURE WINDOW BOOKS
a capstone imprint

It's a busy day on the farm!
Farms provide materials and
food that people use every day.
The milk and eggs on your
breakfast table, and even the
jam and bread, all started out
on a farm.

Farmers milk cows in the
barn, grow vegetables in the
fields, and feed chickens in the
barnyard. With plenty of space
and things to eat, wild animals
make their homes on the farm,
too. From sun up to sun down,
there is so much to see and do!

Contents

The sun creeps up
and dawn light stretches
over the fields of grass
and wheat. Early risers
begin to wake, while other
creatures hide away.

4

The mole uses long claws to dig for a morning meal.

The earthworm wriggles under the ground. He will hide from predators.

Chirp-chirp! A robin's morning song floats across the farmyard.

Can You See?
Field crickets can be a farmer's friend because they eat weeds that could harm their crops. Can you spot the helpful insect?

The rooster
announces the
start of a new day.

The hens
cluck to their
hungry chicks.

Gobble-gobble!
The turkey fans its
tail feathers.

Rise and shine!
A chorus of coos, clucks,
and cock-a-doodle-doos
fills the cool morning air.
The sun is up, and so are
many of the animals.

In the garden,
sunbeams skip
along petals and
vines. Ripe beans
and cabbages soak
up the morning sun.

A bushy-tailed squirrel gathers nuts and seeds.

The bright-winged butterfly sips nectar from a flower.

Hiss! The snake slithers through the shady garden.

Can You See?
Chomp! A caterpillar needs to eat lots of leaves before it can turn into a butterfly. Find the munching caterpillar.

Trot, trot, trot!
Horses run through
the green pasture
as the sun rises
higher in the sky.

The mare
runs with her
playful foal.

This pony
gallops across
the sunny fields.

A friendly
donkey frolics
across the grass.

A hungry goat stretches to reach the feed bag.

High up in a corner, a spider spins a silky web.

Two barn owls snooze. When night falls, they'll hunt for mice.

The farmyard bustles
beneath the bright sun.
In the quiet shade of
the barn, animals eat,
play, and rest.

Can You See?
The field mouse looks for food at night.
For now, it's fast asleep. Do you see it?

The sun is high overhead. It's feeding time for the pigs in their pen.

Pigs and piglets eat corn and wheat for lunch.

The pigs' pen is a good spot for a rat to find food.

Ants carry seeds, insects, and bits of fruit back to their home.

It's a bright afternoon at the pond. Ducks and fish swim and splash. Other animals hide in the shade of the grass.

Ducklings flap their webbed feet back and forth under the water.

A turtle slowly roams the shore looking for roots and berries.

A catfish jumps out of the water. *Splash!*

Can You See?

Ribbit! This small, green amphibian swims with its big eyes sticking out of the water. Can you spy the frog?

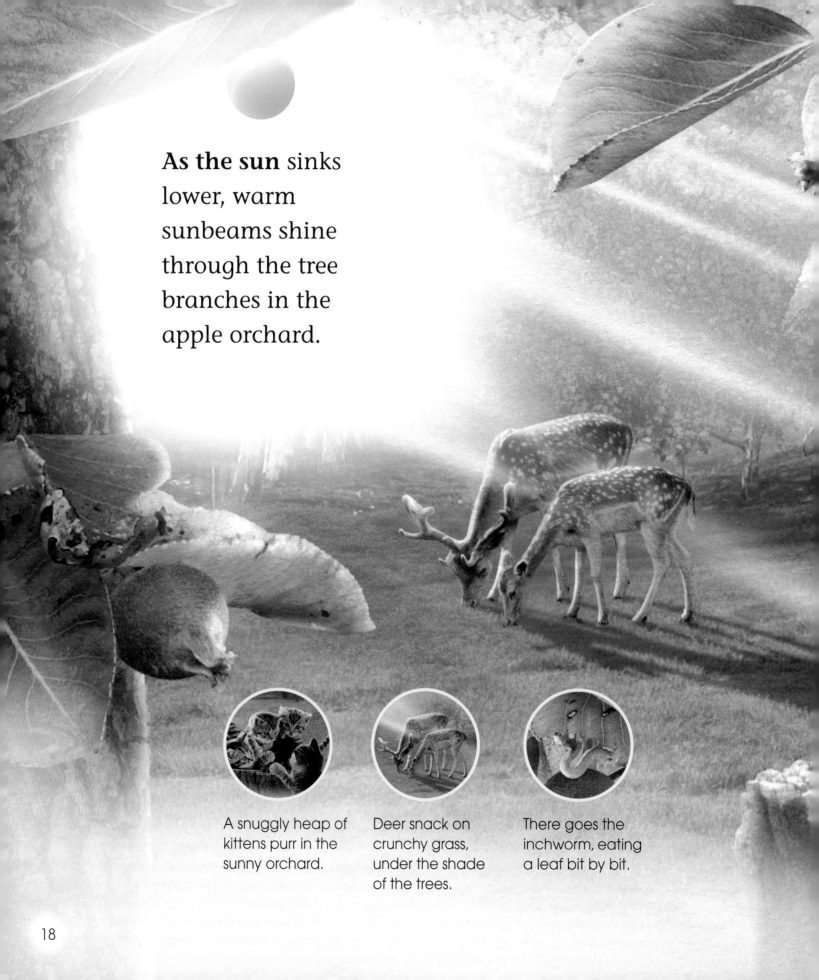

As the sun sinks lower, warm sunbeams shine through the tree branches in the apple orchard.

A snuggly heap of kittens purr in the sunny orchard.

Deer snack on crunchy grass, under the shade of the trees.

There goes the inchworm, eating a leaf bit by bit.

The sun sets
behind the meadow.
An evening glow
spreads over the
fields, where cows
rest in the grass.

High in the sky, a flock of geese fly back to the pond.

Moo, moo! Cows graze on green grass and rest.

Rabbits hop across the meadows. They listen for danger.

21

Hungry bats fly to the orchard for a fruity feast.

The sheepdog guides the sheep into the warm, safe barn.

The woolly flock of sheep will cuddle together and sleep inside the barn.

Dusk settles over the farm. As the moon rises the animals get ready for the night.

Twinkling stars sparkle over the barn, while badgers and foxes hide in the shadows. They'll eat all night and rest when the sun rises.

This badger digs and searches for a snack.

A garden snail glides along a cool, green leaf.

The red fox sips from a stream in the quiet farmyard.

Can You See?

Moths are related to butterflies. They are nocturnal—awake at night. Can you find the insect?

Farm life

Farms are very important. We eat fruit, vegetables, milk, meat, and cheese that come from farms. When we put on clothes made of cotton, wool, or leather, we're wearing things that started on a farm! Take a closer look.

Farmers work hard all year long. There are different jobs to do in each season—from planting and growing to harvesting food.

Butterflies are important to farms because they help gardens to grow.

Rats like to visit pig pens. They have a good memory when it comes to remembering where food can be found.

Foxes like to hunt alone at night. Open fields, such as on a farm, are a good place to find food.

Birds, such as robins, are important visitors. They eat insects that could harm crops.

Cuddly kittens learn to keep grain stores safe from rodents, like mice and rats.

Donkeys can pull small carts or carry heavy loads. Today, most donkeys kept on farms are pets.

Dairy cows are milked twice a day, usually at the very beginning and end of each day.

Fun on the farm

Fun farm facts by the numbers

Some farms grow an important crop called wheat. One bushel of wheat could make around 100 loaves of bread!

Adult turkeys have more than 3,000 feathers.

The wool from one adult sheep is enough to make about five warm sweaters each year.

Mixed-up baby animals

Can you unscramble these
baby animal names?

1. A L F O

2. T N E T K I

3. G U D C L K I N

4. H C I K C

5. G E P I L T

6. I D K

7. F A L C

Glossary

crop:
a plant that can
be grown and harvested

farm:
a piece of land used
for growing crops or
raising livestock

graze:
to feed on growing grass

livestock:
animals kept and raised by
farmers, including horses,
cattle, sheep, and goats

pasture:
plot of land covered with grass
used for grazing

predator:
an animal that hunts and eats
other animals

Index

To Emilio and Cecilia who always work from Sun up to Sun down. — JRD

About the Author

A day in the life of **Joanne Ruelos Diaz** *includes rising before the sun, writing about anything from animals and trains to princesses and fairies, and monkeying around with her little boy. She lives in Brooklyn, NY with her husband and son.*

About the Illustrator

A day in the life of **Simon Mendez** *includes being bounced or shaken awake by his children, drawing and coloring anything and everything he can think of while juggling the family and trying to avoid emails, telephone calls, and real life—then hopefully finding his bed before the sun or the kids rise. He lives in a small village in the North of England with his wife, twins, and Dill the dog.*

Author Joanne Ruelos Diaz
Illustrator Simon Mendez
Designer Winnie Malcolm
Editor Tori Kosara

Published in the United States by
Picture Window Books

Picture Window Books are published by Capstone,
1701 Roe Crest Drive, North Mankato, Minnesota 56003
www.capstonepub.com

Conceived and produced by Weldon Owen Limited
Deepdene Lodge, Deepdene Avenue
Dorking RH5 4AT, UK

Library of Congress Cataloging-in-Publication Data

Diaz, Joanne Ruelos, author.
    Animals on the farm / Joanne Ruelos Diaz.
        pages cm. -- (Animals all day!)
    Summary: "Illustrations and simple text describe a variety of animals, both wild and domestic, on the farm over the course of one day."-- Provided by publisher.
    Includes index.
    ISBN 978-1-4795-5699-1 (hb)
1. Domestic animals--Juvenile literature. 2. Livestock--Juvenile literature. 3. Farm life--Juvenile literature. I. Title.

SF75.5.D525 2014
636--dc23
                                                                    2013049166

ISBN 978-1-4795-5699-1

Printed and bound in China by 1010 Printing Group Limited

135798642